Tempest Feasts, Moon Pies and Me

Check Out Other Titles by LaPortsia Wallace

In This Place And Time
Orange Sunsets
Pocketful of Love

Tempest Feasts, Moon Pies and Me

LaPortsia Wallace

Addax Brillmarre Media

Addax Brillmarre Media Incorporated
2331 Mill Rd., Suite 100, Alexandria, VA 22314

Wallace, LaPortsia.
Tempest Feasts, Moon Pies and Me
ISBN-13 978-0615467191
ISBN-10 0615467199

Introduction

I imagine myself writing poems at a quaint little coffee shop where the service is world class; the coffee is not great but still good served with a cacophony of delicious pies and pie ala modes for my every taste bud. My inspiration comes not so much from the people or the coffee shop itself but from the atmosphere of the place, and my creative juices flow. I can freely verse words into lines and eventually poems. They flow from my pen or my fingers, depending on whether my medium is pen and paper or my laptop. I feel freedom from what I write and within what I write. This life could not have been planned because it is perfect, I am perfect, and my words are forever.

I dedicate this book to those who struggle sometimes on the rollercoaster of life. Life is meant to have its downs, for it makes the ups so much more magical.

Poems

Best

Yellow Flitters

Thomas J.

The Days

An Extraordinary Life

Peaceful Rest

Life's Journey

Breaking Me Free

Moon Pies and Me

Tempest Feasts

I dance in magical array
Of the storms coming back to play
In late August
When tempest feasts
On exhausted summertime treats
We ride back and forth
Across the light
No one can tell us we don't have the right
We look as the children are
When they pranced through September's dawn
The little men invite us in
To sample the fall again
Yet in the late of August nights
When tempest feasts
On what's left of summertime
There are those of us who refuse to retreat
And hear the slow graceful fall of leaves
We dance in magical array
As extraction takes us far away
To diamond ponds, warm and fare
Till tempest appetite is filled for another year.

Here

So many things have changed
Changed me
I make the best
And move on
I smile through
Layers of who I once used to be
But I'm here
No changing that
I'm here
For how ever long it takes
I've got plans
So many plans
But right now I'm here.

Fern Gusts of Wind

Fern gusts of wind
And we ride the trail to the river's edge
Many thousands of years have taken place on this tiny
piece of land
I remember as if it were a dream
The years that have passed and the memories left here
for generations to cherish
The birds and the bees seen in nature
The future of our world
A stroll or a run and we've come to the end of the river
bed
Where life begins
And history is made.

A fossil of a life long gone
Tells me its secrets
And I become one with it
I can sit in one place for more hours in a day
Inspiration finds me
As I jump to the sea
Down a trailing waterfall
In search of so many things
Then fern gusts of wind
Rattle and sway
The tall withering lilacs in fields far away.

Eleven Past

It was eleven past midnight
Storms banged harsh words
Against the window pane
George and I sat up
Back against the wall
Neither one of us daring to move a muscle
The fear encumbered
The dark monster was on the way
It's drooling menace
Drenched the world outside
George and I sat up
Afraid to cry
Trees shook
Timbers uprooted
The ground softened to suck everything within it
I started to shake
A shivering presence made its mark that night
George and I sat up
Listening to the hideous cry
The mournful caroling
The chaotic world at play.

It was eleven past one
A soothing peace caressed the lands
George and I fast asleep
Dreaming away to far away lands
Storms forgotten
Monsters in another place
Sleeping soundly until another day.

I Breathe

In the midst of everything happening
I stand at its center
Its chaos,
I breathe
I sigh
I face the sun and the day
And all that it holds.

I breathe again
And again
It keeps me sane
It keeps me here
It keeps me geared to live another day.

PTRP

Raging winds are all around
I really want to scream
This messy world
I'm imprisoned to
Pushes me to the depths
It's this place they call PTRP
It's sucking the life out of me
Sucking away my moral dreams
And my hopes of one day being
A successful polite citizen
In this great world we live.

Wind Song Raptures

Faith invites the lonely in
Hope invites them all to sing
The beauty of the day
The silence of the night

And wind slowly plays

Right makes the stage a lonely place
Wrong makes the mistakes we don't want to face
In course to life
We will be saved

And wind slowly waits

Her life is green
Like Scrooge McFay
No love of life
No life of love

And wind slowly fades

The wind slowly raps its song to the day
Tap, Tap, Rap
Rap, Tap, Tay
Faith is renewed
And hope is refueled
In the beauty of a day
With a song in June

A stage door opens
To those who wait
No mistakes can be made
With the wind as your mate

In the silence of the night
Reason slowly creeps with
And no decisions are made
Just the silence of the wind song raptures at play.

My Way

Anger
Frustration
The feeling of being trapped
The feeling of not being free
That is what I am feeling now
These days
This year
I know there is a way out
A light at the end of this dark and tumultuous tunnel
I can see it
I can feel it
I can almost touch it
Yet--
--It is still out of my reach.

I know what I should do
With this life given me

--I've always known

Why then am I still here fighting for the privilege to be
me
This is my life isn't it
I shall do with it what I will
I shall climb that mountain over and over again
Until I reach the snow peaked sound
Then I'll know I'm where I'm suppose to be
Because I did it my own way.

Life Out of Me

I run the risk of injuring
The better part of me
By being around those people
Who are draining the life out of me.

The Rain Fell

The rain fell heavy
Heavy in my soul
I couldn't shake the dark clouds
Swirling all around

The rain fell misty
And covered my eyes
No tears can fall today
Even though I'm running out of time
Can we stop the marching hands from racing around the
clock?
Can we stop the rain from falling heavy on my heart?
I want to break the walls
Surrounding my wounded pride
And step up to the plate
Ready to play a great nine

The rain fell heavy
Heavy in my soul
The dark clouds reminding me
To take one day at a time.

Perfect Beauty

The smell of the roses
Bring me wide-eyed into consciousness
I breathe hard
For I may not have the chance again to smell beauty at
its best
I don't want to think awful thoughts especially on such
a beautiful day

But this world makes me sick
I breathe hard
For the beauty is only a mask
And will not last
Why doesn't it stay awhile and play with my
imagination
I hate this world and all it stands for
Yet I love the possibilities it gives me
The opportunity it shares with me especially when love
struts its flare
I want to get out of this rut
I've gotten myself in
So that I can breathe easier
And sing and dance to the wind's melody
Find the sunshine's rays on my face once again
I want to smell the roses
And not have to fear
That it's only for this moment
That life stands still
And gives me all the pleasures of a life in perfect
beauty.

No More

Whilst the room spins round and round
I look to the sky for further insight
Such dark skies and lonely lights
Know my agony and all that's inside
Star light, Star bright
First star I see tonight…
All the while life is passing me by

Sadness has a place in my earth toned soul
I'd like to think it inspires the best in me
But lonely hearts and broken dreams inspire nothing but
idle feet
Open the window to the cool nights breeze
Fill my soul with purpose; meaning
Let me wake the sleeping giant
He who holds my futures delight
And if the room finally stops its turn
Music will come sweeping from my every pore
And to the dark skies
I'll look once more
An offering to give
And my life is no more.

The Storms

The storms still rise up in my heart these days
As more and more anger flourishes there
I find it hard sometimes
To conceal the rage manifesting inside one so young of
age
I cry at those times
When I know that evil is so very near
I curse the world and all its minions
I can't fight the fight I was meant to win
It becomes a prophecy I'm not willing to fulfill.

I can't seem to find comfort much anymore
I curl up in a ball full of despair
I want to die
Leave this world to those whose hearts aren't frozen
over with ice
I want to die
So that the heavens don't have to be ashamed of all the
lies
So my father can rest easy that I hurt no more
So that my mother can remember me before the evil me
morphed.

It's so cold and the air hurts my lungs
I cry out to be saved by anyone
The storms get louder and heavier and longer
And it cuts my world in long deep wounds
I am no more free to roam this land
No more privileged to understand
No more angered by evil doings
I am numb
Like the bullet that takes the life of an innocent child
And is no more.

Still I hope
And sometimes I dream
And the world isn't as bad as I make it out to be
I hunger for the knowledge that will set me free
I itch for the power to simply be me
And the storm of my heart ceases its raging winds
The flowers begin their bloom again
I'm at peace with the world for the time being
And life goes on as if it never changed.

Oil Fields

Stumbling fields of blue and green
Rivers of light
Almost blinding

I awaken succumb to feeling bad
Realization of this life
Makes me sad
I hide the pain
That no one understands
To feel sane is my greatest plan.
At the bus stop
I watch life move like a dance
I'm on the outside
Looking in through panes of glass
Darkness hides it self in my light
Eclipsing my goodness, my sanity.

These days I fight to be content with who I am
To be happy that I can freely laugh
I feel a lot like a river bed
Running in burning oil fields
On grains of sand.

Rose Water

Rose water springs eternal
Or is it eternal springs rose water
Perhaps something like that
Or not at all.
Yet rose and water as one
Make something sweet and magical
I am embraced by such imaginings that bring silliness
to the forefront of me
It makes my world go round
Brings peace to my soul
Freedom to my being.
I am rose water
The very beginning and the end
Sweet and magical
Eternal and ever rising
Like spring.

Songs From the Heart

A golden sunset in the month of May
So vast a day has gone away
With all the hustle, running and change
My heart takes a leap and with triumph skips a beat.

A solitary moment
Is all one needs
To sort through life's many uncertainties
With days gone by
And nights kept kind.

When thoughts of you come rushing by
I keep in mind that love is blind
At the setting of the day,
As the moon beams radiate
I take a deep breath
And my heart takes its place.

When I said I'll love you
Past the stars and the stripes
In balance with forever
I'm in balance with time.

Reaching for the words
I softly sing
Of loves gone by
A child's melody

Repeat to my heart
Gray days and cool nights
The songs of our lifetime come swiftly and part.

Like the songs of my heart
And the days of my life.

The Mark of Excellence

The mark of excellence is easy to see
Especially in someone like you.

The rivers open wide
And mountains stand tall
When they see you passing by.

The weight of the world sits comfortably on your
shoulders
For it sees all you shall be
--All the beauty and majesty
That will take you places unseen.

A day will come when moonbeams and stars
Dance upon your light
As you revel in the moment of your oh too perfect life.

Remember these times
For they are special in what shall eventually be
Treasure friends, family, and others
Who support your every move.
Be all you can be
A cliché to say the least
But one born in truth.

For you--
The seas will rise
In wondrous ovation
At all that you shall be
Excellent beyond imagining
A success because you believe.

I Am Sorry

What words do I come up with
To say that I am sorry
For all the wrong things said
None for the right reasons
I am on a leash of indecision
My hesitation profound
Especially in light of my words not coming out sound
I pass into the sedimentary night abyss of wanting to
take it back
Start over again
But I am willed to the strongest of men
To keep my resolve placed where it is
I never know the consequences of my words
Until they have reached their intended mark
I apologize irreverently for not thinking first
For fear of insanity made me markedly rush
I am weakened by it
For friendship is lost
And the consequences forever will stain my heart.

Winter's Slumberland

Petals of flowers fall
I imagine day is night
Fire blazing warm
Engulfing my mind
Winter need not come this year
For summer was all a wash
I sink in myself
And remember what was lost
Things I can't remember
Words never said
A summer of frantic days
A summer unspent
Wasted
Literally
To the crouching wind
Who blows the petals falling
Off to winter's slumberland.

Sunday Afternoon

Vinelines tether to the tune
The clouds run skylight interference
Choral voices can clearly be heard
In the random background of what beauty has restored
Magnificent aromas rise to mountain peaks
The world as we know it
Is bending backward over knee
Lemon drop poppies
Gayford Sams
Oak laced treasures
Invite only the heartfelt in
To private parties
And licorice stands.

All comical amusements reach no end
As windy rainbows take flight and sail away
Edge line memories
Are mostly what we stand
Around alp climbing sabertooths
Minding their land
Youthful thoughts are the keys to this world
Whether you understand them fully or not
On hot Sunday afternoons.

My Window Ledge

The skyscraped peaks
Call my name
They whisper my future
In the cool breezed air
Peace it seems
Has filled the lands
As snow falls softly on my window ledge.

The Strength of Determination

The light hits me in the oddest places
At the oddest times
And I can't get a proper grip on reality
The cesspool of my consciousness is muddy
With so many things left undone
Will I finish before my time expires?
That is my biggest worry
My biggest fear
What if I should die before I wake
What if I should lose all insight
Before I can make my mark on this world
What if…
What if…
So many worries
So many fears
But I have determination
I know I have it within me to be something
Someone
Great
And I will achieve all that has been given to me

I guess it is simply a matter of time
A matter of patience
A matter of the heart
The passion I have climbs up my throat sometimes
And I'm filled to the brim
With things I will do
Disappointment overwhelms me
And brings me into the depths of hell
When I fail to achieve that which has been given so
generously to me
But I always overcome
And redecorate that ghoulish hell
I want to thank inspiration for giving me my gift

The courage of imagination
The strength of determination
And the seeds of passion
I will do right by my creations
And give back that which has been given to me
And make sure the light that hits me in the oddest
places
At the oddest times
Touches the world
So that it too may be free to grip life's reality.

Dog Race

I'm back in the dog race
Running circles round them
Them, the ones who said I'd never have a chance
Broken and beaten
Tired of their play
I surpassed the competition
With my hearts light glowing red
When you set your mind to something
Things happen or they don't
But when one sets their heart to it
There's nothing that can't be won
So yes, I'm back in the dog race
And my head high in the clouds
Winning all the races
With my heart wearing the crown.

Free

Free once
Yes we were
To soar beyond the moonlit sky
Far away lands would call us home
Call us home to be free once more.

With My Eyes Closed

The spiraling shiny stairway
That rises to its occasion
Has feet like wings
And hands like candy
It sings soul songs
That enrich lost days
When he walks to my door
Then nothing else can take the place
Of warm feelings in December
And creamy whipples of gray
Long respect is claimed on days like this
Dreams come true beyond the grave
With my eyes closed so can we make haste
Up the shiny stairway
That rises to eternity.

Best

Windy hollows awake in bloom
And I can't help but think of how I got here
Once in friendships carriage
Beneath a ripe apple tree
Telling secrets we've told no one else
A bond so holy at best
I can't think of anyone who rode with me here but you.
You are the best in every sense
The best even at your worst
When I think of friends past and present
You are the one I think of best.

Yellow Flitters

Yellow flitters on warm afternoons
I remember things the way they should have been
Days like thick molasses
And nights like goat's milk

Love fills the air

Dancing daises fill my head
With the sweetest song
That taste like marmalade
My heart marks the air
With peace of mind

Love fills the air

I will never stop loving thee
You remind me of being in a dream
Like miracles of life on warm afternoons
Yellow flitters coo
With remembrances of me and you

Still love fills the air.

Thomas J.

They say his name
I hear it whispered
In the fields here and there
Respect
Hate
Love.
He no longer walks amongst us
Yet the air is thick with his presence
He roams the battlefields
He once stood upon
Sadness fills his spiritual being
So many
So young
Gone before life had a chance to embrace them.

It is the reality
The agony
--Of War
It is war that compels misery to speak its truth
--Its of human vanity
Human sacrifice
Human hate
Human sorrow

But also
Human love.

Our past is past
And we cannot get it back
Time makes me mindful of the greatness of man
Even in his ugliest hour.

I cannot fault the past for times were different
We know so much more now than we did in those ages

Dark? Perhaps
Un-enlightened? In some cases
Educated differently
To a belief that sometimes amazes me
But to find fault, I simply cannot.

I embrace the past
I embrace him
He gives me light
And I walk in his belief
His faith and love
His courage and perseverance
He is my history to hold
For as long as I can
To pass and to mold
As a life we should not deny
--Not for reasons of war anyway.

I stand here
--Nearly one hundred and fifty years gone
They say his name still
I sit and I listen
Intently—
Respectfully—
For he is my hero of past
My secret confidant
Despite a war that separated man from mankind
Brother from brother
Nation from nation—

--I am honored
In any case.

The Days

The days seem never ending
I stop at the river's edge
Afraid that I'll jump right in
The wind keeps me cool
I feel love in its gentle touch
I am banished to this land
Not quite sure where to go.
I look to the sun for guidance
The dark clouds hover about
Night may be falling
But my heart is still aglow
I take some comfort that there will be another day
I take some comfort
That I may find you standing
Waiting to guide me away
Far away
Where I can breath deep the fresh free air
Far away
Where the day closes its eyes to the stars shinning gaze
I make my self comfortable on the river's edge
I can see my reflection
In the rippling shade
Am I at peace in this parallel world?
Or am I dreaming of good days to come?
The days they seem never ending
I slide to the edge
And see forever
The coolness invites me for one quick swim
I'm afraid of drowning
And losing the day
The pied pipers song rings through my ears
And I make a decision never to be unhappy again
I rise to my feet
Heart racing to my throat

Outstretch my hands
And simply let go
To the day never ending
And the river its mighty sword
We close our eyes together
And find peace in those we love.

An Extraordinary Life

The rag-a-muffins have trapped me here
They have rung me out to dry
I breath deep
I sigh relentlessly
I am at a loss for progression
I am a lower version of my true self
Unable to see the power of me
To know that I am truly free
I have always been free
I was born free.

From this moment
I must promise myself I shall love free
So that I may die free
And know that I have lived an extraordinary life.

Peaceful Rest

I love swallow's eve's
And milky sunsets
When the world at its best
Lays down to peaceful rest

Life's Journey

The road I'm traveling on
Is long and harsh
Sometimes I don't think
I'll ever find a resting spot
But then
I look at you with your smile so bright
I look at you
Your eyes so full of life
I look at you
Love.

The path I'm taking
On my way back home
Is constant with distractions, detours and such
I try hard to keep my head out of the stars
Knowing the stumbling might cause me some harm
But I see you
At the end of my road
I know you
Because I can feel your love
I hear you whispering
You're almost home.

The journey I'm facing
Makes me scared sometimes
It's like stepping into a field full of mines
But I'm confident and alright
I'm secure knowing I have a purpose in life
I'm fearless
As I walk out my door
On life's road not taken
I'm almost home.

Breaking Me Free

When do we begin to know how this life will turn out?
It is not at our beginning
And I hope it will not be at our end
Somewhere in the middle perhaps?
There must be a moment when a light bulb illuminates
our true path to destiny.

I've sat here
At the tower of indecision
For longer than I'd like to admit
Convinced I'm lost
Unable to make my way through the overgrown forest
of my indecision.
I look out at the abyss
Convinced my path lies just beyond the great fog
Yet I sit and I squint
Adventure
--Less
I am consumed by my misery
Yet there is so much that I desire
I look for the day to come
When I remove myself
From my unforgiving perch
And stand at the crossroads and squint no more
I shall put one foot in front of the other
And confidently walk through the mirage of uncertainty
That silently conceals my future's truth
Where I hope to find my ambitions achieved
And my future revealed as sunny and bright.

Yet how will I know when to take the chance
To pick myself up
Outstretch my arms and feel my way to ultimate
freedom

That which is my life
My destiny
Me revealed
To a world I'm not ready for.

Moon Pies and Me

In the miracles of today
I am grateful for moon pie days
When the best of me is content to linger life away
When the sweetness of moments bring flare and
meaning
When I can see the future and its not so gloomy

I sit upon the rose colored bench of my youth
And dream away the hours to find my truth
This life that I have
A miracle upon itself
Which reminds me of feasts
I've treasured since birth
The red checkered blanket
That rests just off the lands
Holds delicacies of life
Secrets not yet shared

Moon pies of glory
Show their truest in spades
And I reluctantly whisper
My wants to the rain.
In fairy lore
Across sparkling shores
That invite me to live
In its mighty roar
With feasts unimagined
Moon pies galore
I am content with what
Keeps me coming back for more
And I find the peace a revelry these days
As I march
Forever
Moon pies in hand.